# The Golden Boat: Selected Poems of Srečko Kosovel

SREČKO KOSOVEL (1904–1926) was born in Sežana, spent his childhood in the neighbouring village of Tomaj, and was educated in Ljubljana. Often called the Slovenian Rimbaud, he is thought to have written over one thousand poems before his early death, although during his lifetime he published less than forty. Renowned initially for his impressionist lyrics of the Karst region above Trieste, the remarkable modernist component of his work began to be realised only forty years after his death.

BERT PRIBAC is a Slovenian poet and essayist. He studied comparative literature at the University of Ljubljana but in 1959 left Slovenia and after a short period as a refugee in Germany, settled in 1960 in Australia where he eventually became librarian for the Commonwealth Department of Health. He returned to Slovenia in 2003. He is the author of six collections of poetry, and has edited and translated into Slovenian two anthologies of contemporary Australian verse. His most recent publication is a Slovenian translation, from the French, of the *Rubayat* of Omar Khayam. He lives in Istria, about 20 km south of Trieste, where he now tends his vineyard.

DAVID BROOKS is an Australian poet, short-fiction-writer, novelist and essayist whose work has been translated into several languages. He is married to the Slovenian photographer and translator Teja Pribac and, when not in Slovenia, lives in New South Wales where he teaches Australian Literature at the University of Sydney and co-edits the journal *Southerly*.

# The Golden Boat

## SELECTED POEMS OF SREČKO KOSOVEL

*Translated by*

BERT PRIBAC & DAVID BROOKS

*with the assistance of* TEJA BROOKS PRIBAC

SALT

CROMER

PUBLISHED BY SALT PUBLISHING
12 Norwich Road, Cromer, Norfolk NR27 0AX, United Kingdom

Salt Publishing 2008, 2011

Printed and bound in the United Kingdom by Lightning Source UK Ltd

Typeset in Swift 9.5 / 13

ISBN 978 1 84471 437 7 hardback
ISBN 978 1 84471 855 9 paperback

1 3 5 7 9 8 6 4 2

# Contents

# Srečko Kosovel: Life and Poetry

Srečko Kosovel (1904–1926) is frequently called the Slovenian Rimbaud. The two are very different poets, but the comparison is understandable. There is, for example, their youth: Kosovel died at twenty-two, and while Rimbaud (1854–1893) in fact reached thirty-nine, he supposedly gave up the writing of poetry at somewhere between twenty and twenty-two years of age. And there is their productivity: if the volume of work Rimbaud produced between the ages of sixteen and twenty is impressive, the volume of Kosovel's work is astonishing. People speak of his having left almost a thousand poems, and while at least half of these are of contestable status—drafts, rather than poems, or pieces too fragmentary to be called poems at all—at least five hundred of them have been published as achieved poems in the eighty years since his death, and to these we should add numerous articles and other pieces, and a large quantity of letters.

There is, too, the delayed recognition and publication of their writing. Rimbaud published only a handful of poems before abandoning the art, and although he did prepare one publication, his landmark *A Season in Hell* (*Un Saison en Enfer*), he could not pay the bill and left almost the entire edition at the printer's premises (where they were discovered in 1901—almost thirty years later—by a Belgian lawyer). Kosovel, in his turn, published less than forty poems during his lifetime, and while he did put together a collection, *The Golden Boat* (*Zlati Čoln*), in the hopes of publication, this was rejected by the intended publisher and did not appear until 1954—arguably did not even appear then, since the selection of poems which appeared under that title was not in fact Kosovel's own.

There is also war, and the horror of war, and the impact upon their writing and their creative psyche of their early exposure to these things. Rimbaud's native village, Charleville, was near the battlefront in the Franco-Prussian War of 1870–71—or, rather, the battlefront came very near to it, a matter of a few kilometres—and his *floreat* coincided with the Siege of Paris. Tomaj, the village in which Kosovel spent most of his childhood, was little more than twenty kilometres, as the crow flew, from the Isonzo (the Soča River), one of the worst battlefields of the First World War. It was also the site of a field hospital. Each poet, that is to say—Rimbaud in his middle teens, and Kosovel just as his teens began—would have seen troops marching through his village to the nearby battlefront, and the dead, dying and wounded being carried away. At one point Charleville was actually bombarded, and if Tomaj escaped bombardment, Dutovlje, the village next to it, was not so lucky. If Kosovel was not raped by soldiers, as it is thought Rimbaud had been, he had certainly, before his parents sent him and his sister to Ljubljana, seen corpses. And in each case this war is at once the result and the origin of wider social upheaval, so that each poet can be seen to be the site and register of considerable political and intellectual conflict, a conflict that stimulates their reshaping of the very art that it compels. Each, in his own way, is an artistic avant-guardist, the origin, within his own tradition, of a new way of writing, at an age at which most other poets have not even begun to flower.

Yet temperamentally they are not so close. One cannot imagine that Srečko Kosovel ever drank very much absinthe (indeed the Slovenian poem, as he sees it, is dying from its 'heavy intoxication'), and while he without doubt sees himself, and can be seen—in his sense of nationhood, and of the Slovenian nation in particular—as something of a visionary, this does not at first appear to reach, as it does in Rimbaud (albeit in broad brush-strokes), quite so evidently into the structure of thought itself: there is in Kosovel no theory or praise of excess, no 'systematic deregulation of the senses'. He is, one suspects, more disciplined, more earnest, more keen to *achieve* his vision than is Rimbaud—works harder, and arguably within a narrower imaginative range. Although there are poems enough that have a striking energy and power, there is no *tour de force* like *Le bateau ivre* in Kosovel; the images do not pour out upon one another with the same kind of surreal intensity, and the satire, when it comes (and it does come, fluently), has its own edge, different from the vituperation and the scatological that one finds so often in Rimbaud. The striking images, like the satirical barbs, are there, but they appear in contexts that enable and encourage us to look at them closely, rather than (to caricaturise Rimbaud [one could also speak of 'explosive tumult']) jostle one another like a conga line across a stage. None of which is to suggest that Kosovel did not know of Rimbaud, or admire him, or have him sometimes in mind. Bert Pribac recalls that Kosovel had at least one literary friend in Paris (Peter Martinc), who communicated regularly with him, and there are signs aplenty within the work itself—the force and recurrence of the boat and the sea in the poetry, for example, and even (in 'The Sail', 'A Face at the Window') the occasional focus upon sailors amidst the wild raging of the sea—that suggest not only a knowledge but even, perhaps, a referencing of and positioning in regard to *Le bateau ivre*.

But Rimbaud is not the only comparison to be made, and to dwell upon it, helpful as it can be, also biasses the picture. On first encountering his earlier, 'Impressionist' poems, seeding as they do the rituals and landscape of the Karst with oblique references to the wider events that are reshaping it, an English reader might think of the work of Edward Thomas, and an Australian of the strong, simple rural lyrics of David Campbell. But I mean something other than this. Kosovel was born into a rich force-field of creativity. Another way to see him and to explain some of his quality and significance is to look at him in his own time and geographical situation. Slovenian commentators have always done this, and argued Kosovel's place amongst other Slovenian poets of significance such as France Prešeren, Ivan Cankar and, closer to our own moment, Dane Zajc and Tomaz Šalamun. This, especially given Kosovel's own spiritual sense of the Slovenian nation, is perfectly understandable, and there is strong reason to see Kosovel as standing at the centre of this group, but to see him only in this light is to corral him.

Hard as it is to know quite what to make of it, it is worth considering that two of the greatest literary works of the twentieth century, in any language—Joyce's *Ulysses*, and Rilke's *Duino Elegies*—were conceived and substantially written within a few kilometres of Tomaj. Joyce came to live in Trieste in 1904, the year in which Kosovel was born in a village on the plateau above it, and lived there—a period in Zurich, during the war, aside—until 1920, when, in the face of nascent fascism and the repression of the Slovene 'minority' (30% of the population of Trieste itself, 95% in the countryside around it), he felt that the spirit of the city had changed—the artistic freedom gone out of it—and moved to Paris. During his time in Trieste, however, he had written most of the stories of *Dubliners*, and *A Portrait of the Artist as a Young Man*, and almost all of *Ulysses*.

Rilke similarly. It was in Duino, in late January 1912, at the castle of Countess Marie von Thurn und Taxis-Hohenlohe, that Rilke—walking the battlements, overlooking the sea, or perhaps in a cliff path below the castle wall (the story varies) in a high wind—first 'heard' the opening of the first elegy, and spent the rest of the day in furious composition. Duino (*Devin*) is on the Adriatic coast, just a few kilometers to the west of Trieste. It's not recorded what Joyce was doing that day, nor of course what the almost eight-year-old Kosovel was doing—we can see them, geographically, as corners of a small isosceles triangle—but the wind was almost certainly the notorious *burja* ('Bora', or 'Boria'), infamous from ancient times (Catullus mentions it), which blows directly southward from the Alps, only forty kilometers northward at this point and visible, fog allowing, every day of the year. The *burja*, much like the Mistral further to the west, has the reputation for making people irritable beyond measure, to the point where it becomes almost a psychic force. It has a particularly strong presence in Kosovel. One of his finest poems, the almost-untranslatable 'Pines' ('*Bori*') plays significantly upon its name, the pines and the wind that blows through them becoming inextricable, a part, quite literally, of one-another's definition.

How much Kosovel knew of Joyce's work is not clear, though given their proximity and the size of the Triestine literary and artistic community—while living in Tomaj, Bert Pribac has written, 'Kosovel went almost regularly to Trieste with his sister and aunts to attend opera and theatre, both in Slovene and Italian environments. Kosovel not only breathed the same *burja* as Joyce, but tasted the same cultural milieu as well'—it is unlikely that he would not have known of him. Rilke seems to have been something else again. His work was readily available, and Kosovel would have had no difficulty reading him in the original. Not only was German his first language after Slovenian, but there was his sister Karmela, a pianist, in Munich (where Rilke had spent most of the war), to send him books that might not have been available locally. If Rilke's 'Autumn Day', 'Autumn' and 'The End of Autumn' were not, as they can sometimes seem, high amongst Kosovel's favourite poems (some of his numerous *Jesen* [Autumn] poems seem to look directly at Rilke's), and *Das Buch der Bilder* (1902) one of his favourite contemporary works, then the frequent similarity in titles and images perhaps testifies to a more significant dialogue, and might help us come a little closer to understanding something of the specific quality and force of Kosovel's lyricism.

And Joyce and Rilke are hardly the sum of it. The war had brought other writers to and out of the region. It's a common misconception that Hemingway, for example, fought—or, rather, saw action, since he was an ambulanceman, not a soldier—at the Isonzo/Soča front, whereas in fact he saw it, and was wounded, on the Piave River, a few kilometers futher to the west. By the time he arrived in Italy (1918), the Isonzo front had gone quiet; all the battles of the Isonzo are between 1915 and 1917; but he was close enough to hear sufficient of it to have Henry, the central character of *A Farewell to Arms* (1929), wounded there, and saw enough of the landscape at close hand to make it part of his creative imagination.

Closer to Kosovel in a different sense is the Italian poet, Giuseppe Ungaretti, who fought on the Isonzo and wrote some of his most memorable poetry about the experience. The harsh contours of the Karst seem, unobtrusively, to underpin the austere, almost minimalist concentration of his poems, giving them in their turn contours very like those of Kosovel's strangely mis-named 'Impressionist' work, in which he is most concerned to describe and capture that landscape.

Voluntarily or otherwise, however, these were all visitors. If they drew from the place, as each of them most certainly did—from the horrors perpetrated there, as well as from what we might speak of as a kind of cold and flinty spiritual force—it was only Kosovel who was born and grew up there and attempted to speak directly of its power.

~

The youngest of five children, Srečko Kosovel—Srečko (pronounced *Sretch-ko*) means 'lucky' or 'fortunate' in Slovenian (Kosovel would at times call himself 'Felix')—was born on March 18, 1904, in Sežana, not in Tomaj, to which smaller town, eight kilometres away (and closer to the Soča) the family moved in 1908 when his father was appointed headmaster of its elementary school. Srečko spent nearly eight years in Tomaj before, at almost twelve, he was sent with his sister Anica to Ljubljana for further schooling, a move that must have been difficult for the young children, who were barely into their teens, but which had the decided advantage of placing them further away from the war. Thereafter, school and university holidays aside, Kosovel was to spend the rest of his life in Ljubljana, now the capital of Slovenia but then a large provincial town near the southern extremity of the Austro-Hungarian Empire.

Slovenia did not at this point exist as a separate political entity. The Slovenian people, their language and their culture, were a different matter, but political autonomy awaited the end of the war and the redistribution of the Empire of the Habsburgs. Even then it was not a clean or swift process. Slovenia became part of the Kingdom of the Serbs, Croats and Slovenes, but this Slovenia did not coincide with the geographical distribution of Slovenian cultural and linguistic hegemony. Kosovel's region, to the west, was in dispute, Istria and the Karst in particular. This was in part because of the highly desirable seaport of Trst (Trieste), and the lesser ports of Koper (Capodistria) and Piran (Pirano) to the southeast of it on the present-day Slovene coast, but perhaps in larger part to the cultural integrity of Istria—a hybrid integrity, if we can speak of such a thing: Mediterranean, where the rest of Slovenia is Alpine and sub-Alpine, and bearing the imprint of an association, as long as recorded history, with the Italian peninsular and culture, and more specifically with Venice, just across the water (the great trees of the once densely-forested Karst provided the hardwood piers of Venice; the doges used Pirano as a hunting-lodge and source of wine; much of the marble of Venice is Istrian). Following the war, and while treaties were being negotiated, Italy had interim control of Trieste and its surrounds. The 1920 Treaty of Rapallo, between Italy and the Kingdom of the Serbs, Croats and Slovenes, by which the latter was forced to give up Istria and the entire Slovenian and Croatian coastlines, confirmed this, and emergent fascism in Italy gave it a brutal force. In 1920 the Slovenian National House (*Slovenski Narodni Dom*) in Trieste was burned in an arson attack; teaching in the Slovene language was phased out in schools from 1923; in 1925 the Slovene community bank in Trieste was closed down; by 1927, the year after Kosovel's death, it was forbidden to speak Slovenian in public.

I have mentioned the Karst, a region that does not coincide with Istria, but which in part overlaps, in part lies behind and above it. The term 'karst' refers at once to a particular kind of rock and set of rock formations ('a type of topography that is formed over limestone, dolomite or gypsum by solution of the rock and is characterized by closed depressions or sinkholes, caves and underground drainage'), and to the Kras region—a range of mountains between Slovenia and Italy—which most distinctively present this kind of topography. Fourty-four percent of Slovenia is classified Karst, albeit of several types and regions: the Alpine Karst, the Dinaric Karst, etc.. In the sense that it is the region that gave these other types their name, Kosovel's Karst is the original, Litorral Karst, a plateau, largely of limestone, three of the most impressive physical features of which are an escarpment of white cliffs that, with some intervals, overlooks and runs the length of the Istrian coast; an extensive network of limestone caves (some of the most impressive in the world); and a rather harsh and infertile landscape above them: it is said that most of the water that falls on the Karst goes immediately underground, to feed a huge network of subterranean rivers, lakes and springs, leaving the inhabitants of the land above to struggle with poor and unproductive soil, battered for a third of the year by the *burja* as they do so. Rock farmers, some have called them, since stones, boulders and rockfaces are one of the most characteristic features of its fields. Some of the most characteristic products of the region are marked in one way or another by this very harshness: its red wines, grown from the *refosk* grape, such as the famous *Teran*, so harsh and astringent (until one acquires the taste for it: it has a high lactic acid content) that Joyce described it as the perfect wine to serve one's enemies, and its famous prosciutto, said to acquire its particular flavour from the *burja* in which it was traditionally dried. This particular turbulent period in Istrian and Slovenian history, and the place of the Karst as foil to and central character within it, impacted deeply upon Kosovel. One could say that his poetry has one face to this landscape, as a kind of anchor, as he turns the other to the political instability and cultural oppression that surround and wash over it. His father, Anton, a schoolteacher, choirmaster, and ardent Slovenist—in Tomaj he taught in Slovene—was from the Vipava valley, just a little to the north, and his mother Katerina from a town on the Soča River, although, before her marriage, she had been living in Trieste. They were, this is to say, very much a family of the region. When Kosovel went to Ljubljana for his high school education, for example, he was sent to the Technical High School rather than the Gymnasium, in part for financial reasons but in part also in the expectation that he would study either engineering or forestry, and contribute to the rebuilding and reforestation of the denuded Karst. It has been said that the Treaty of Rapallo was one of the tragedies of his short life.

Certainly one can see how it, and its unfolding consequences, galvanised his aesthetic. Grief, loss, anger, displacement, and the passion they evoke, are some of the strongest sources of poetry. Kosovel's early work—if one can speak of such stages in so short a writing life—has been termed 'Impressionist' and is frequently criticised and discounted, in the face of the more demonstrably avant garde later work, as nostalgic or sentimental. But that, I think, is a regional criticism, mounted for regional reasons. Another way of approaching this early work is to see it as imagistic and its concentration about a certain core of diction, emotions and physical features as symbolising and encoding its landscape. To place it in the light of turn-of-the-century Yeats, of Pound's imagism, and of the T'ang poetry that lies behind the latter, but perhaps first and foremost in the light of Rilke, is to bring out colours in Kosovel that a consideration within a more exclusively Slovenian or even central European tradition might not reveal. It introduces, for example (*a la* Rimbaud again), free verse to its region, just as, later, Kosovel would introduce the prose poem.

In the meantime, however, he has also introduced something else. Kosovel's 'Impressionist' poetry is frequently referred to as such in order to contrast it with his 'Expressionist' or 'Constructivist' work. While it is clear that there is an energy, a topicality, a satiric force, an almost-painterly sense of collage, and a delight in typography in the purportedly Expressionistic or Constructivist poems that can remind us at one and the same time of the *Calligrammes* of Apollinaire, of Kurt Schwitters, and of Marinetti's futurism (to the sentiments of which, nonetheless, Kosovel was largely opposed), and that this can be a far cry from the calm, sometimes almost sombre, chiaroscuric quality of the early Karst poetry, to separate them too distinctly and automatically is to ignore the extent to which the latter is prefigured in the former, and the former continues in the latter, as if the latter has come to join and envigorate rather than replace it. What, after all, *is* Constructivism? While there can be no doubt that Kosovel knew something of Russian Constructivism, for example—Naum Gabo's 'Realistic Manifesto', which introduced the term and the theory, was published in 1920 and by 1925 Constructivism had become a significant movement in post-revolutionary Russian aesthetics—he is hardly constrained by it, but reflects an amalgam of avant guard poetic trajectories (Dada, Futurism, Surrealism) which cannot comfortably be tied down to any definition other than the poet's own. Kosovel's Constructivism, the central product of which is a number of poems entitled 'Kons' ('Kons', Kons. 5', 'Kons: ABC', etc.), seems in fact, in the months before his death, to have been superceded by a further understanding of what he called 'extreme' poetry, in the series he referred to as his Integrals.

This rapid development reflects a mind thirsty for new information, driven by a sense of urgency and evolving purpose. As evidenced by his repeated attempts to edit, found or appropriate a magazine or journal through which he could promulgate his own and sympathetic ideas—he edited a magazine called *Lepa Vida* (*Beautiful Vida*), for example, at the age of eighteen, and in 1925, having projected various other magazines which never quite got off the ground (a constructivist journal to be called *Konstrukter*, a literary monthly to be called *Volja* [*Will*]), took over the Slovene

Farmers' Association magazine for young people, *Mladina* (*Youth*), which he then set out to radicalise—Kosovel clearly saw himself as a leader, or potential leader, in the poetry and poetics of his region. More than this, he saw himself as performing, through his poetry and poetics, a role in the encouragement and development of what he saw as a 'new man', a new mode of human being—a concept much in the air and the nature of which was much in contention. Appal at Italian fascism and apprehension concerning the imperial ambitions of Serbia in the Kingdom of the Serbs, Croats and Slovenes had rendered him deeply sceptical of political nationalism, and his attempt to synthesise a spiritual concern for the Slovene nation in abstract, a political anti- and inter-nationalism, and a concern for people against state, had drawn him more and more strongly towards socialism, and stimulated more and more strongly the search for an accompanying aesthetic. This led him into Constructivism, and then, in the attempt to move on from this, into what has come to be called his Zenitism, by which is meant his engagement with ideas promulgated by *Zenit* (Belgrade/Zagreb), then one of the leading avant garde literary journals in Europe, and eventually, having come to the conviction that the kind of formal and stylistic experimentation in which he had been engaged should not take precedence over the greater revolution in human society and the shape of contemporary man, to the more politicised and left-wing poetry of his final phase—a poetry which, as I have been suggesting, does not so much supplant as come to joint the styles and subjects which had characterised his earlier work.

It has taken some time for this trajectory to become apparent to Kosovel's readers. As stated earlier, only forty of his poems were published during his lifetime, and although a first selection of sixty-six of his poems appeared 1927, a further selection in 1931, and a more extensive collection in 1947, it was not until 1967, forty-one years after his death, that the bulk of the Kons and Integrals poems were released. This collection, entitled *Integrali '26*, established him at last as a revolutionary modernist and gave him a significant place in Slovenian literary history. It has also led to some interesting confusion. The combination of the fact that most of his constructivist and later 'extreme' poetry has had to be transcribed from manuscripts which Kosovel himself never had the opportunity to convey into print, and the sense that he was, at the time at which he wrote them, clearly inclined to experiment with typography and visual effects and displacements on the page, has led to a measure of second guessing on the part of his later interpreters, not all of whom have been able to resist the temptation to render ambiguities in his poems visually or to in other ways present him, typographically, in the way they imagine he might have presented himself. While in all likelihood Kosovel might have been delighted at their interpretations, and while it does appear that he left some hints and instructions in this regard, it remains a fact that, in this sense at least, a certain amount of Kosovel's work seems to have been translated in the very act of presenting it, even in his own language, and that those who would translate him into other languages should bear this in mind.

Those readers who would like to see a wider range of the Kons and Integrals poems are referred to two excellent Slovenian publications, an English edition of the aforementioned *Integrals* that appeared as issue 2 of *Litterae Slovenicae (Slovenian Literary Magazine)* in 1998, translated by Nike Kocijančič Pokorn, Katarina Jerin and Philip Burt, and a later, delux version of a selection of the same translations, with a few new translations added: *Man in a Magic Square* (Ljubljana: Mobitel, 2004). An earlier introduction to many of these pieces was offered by William Heiliger, who published fifty of Kosovel's poems as *Integrals* in 1983 (Mudborn Press, Santa Barbara) and again in 1989 (Hungry Bear Press, San Francisco). Some individual poems have appeared in international literary journals in excellent English translations by Ana Jelnikar, Erica Johnson Debeljak and others. An invaluable resource for this present collection has been *Srečko Kosovel: Ikarjev Sen (Srečko Kosovel: The Dream of Icarus)*, an extensive selection of facsimile reproductions of his poems in manuscript, with a large selection of photographs and other documents (in Slovenian), prepared by Ludwig Hartinger and Aleš Berger, published in Ljubljana by Mladinska Knjiga in 2004.

The poems in this collection have been worked up, in some cases only very slightly, from translations by Bert Pribac, who between 2004 and 2006 completed the monumental task of translating over five hundred of Kosovel's poems into English, and who in 2005 asked me to collaborate in the selection and final polishing of a volume. Teja Pribac—no relative of Bert's, but a translator herself—has been a rich and rigorous fund of advice. Contemporary literary translation is a minefield. Some of the issues are clear enough—whether, for example, one attempts to bring the poem to the reader by smoothing out its eccentricities and aiming for the most beautiful (and *familiar*) poem in the target language, or attempts instead to bring the reader to the poem by reproducing as best one can its strangeness and particular character—but the manner in which, in any given locus, one resolves or juggles them is not. In general, on that particular issue, I have taken the latter course—or rather, finding that that is the course that Bert Pribac has taken, have sought to assist it. All virtue in these translations is his and Teja's; any error is most probably mine.

One of the problems facing contemporary translation practice, and a significant inhibition when it comes to the best representation of the poet being translated, is the felt pressure in translators themselves to be original at every point, so as to distinguish their work clearly from that of previous translators of the same text. When the translation of a line or group of lines in a poem is clear—when they move easily into English in a form that is likely to occur to several different people attempting to translate them—then the assumption that the first person to translate them in this manner has somehow copyrighted them and that others must use a different form can only produce less and less effective translation. In major authors whose work is translated many times, this can become almost a principle of deteriorating translation. We have pursued, in creating our versions of these poems, what has seemed to us the best and (as it has often been) most obvious translation of the original poems. It has not been of concern to us that earlier translators might have made very similar or even identical choices in translating those poems, nor, when we have found this to be the case, have we felt a need to change our own translations.

A note, in closing, about the selection and the order in which the poems appear, and about the particular *manner* in which some of those poems appear. Hitherto the bulk of Kosovel's poems to have appeared in English has been from the *Integrali* (*Integrals*) volume of 1967. Bert Pribac, on the other hand, is Istrian, has had a life-long association with the Karst, and has a particular and contageous interest in and affinity for the earlier, 'Impressionist' poetry in which the region and its landscape feature so strongly. This selection is unique in giving almost as much attention to this poetry as to that of Kosovel's Constructivist and Integrals phases. Its first section, 'The Golden Boat', features this earlier poetry and, with some occasional slight adjustments, follows the order in which Anton Ocvirk orders these poems in the first volume of *Srečko Kosovel: Zbrano Delo* (*Collected Works* [1964]). The second section, 'Integrals', features poems which were first released in Ocvirk's edition of *Integrali* in 1967, and follows his ordering. In the third section we have placed a selection of poems which either first appeared in a 1974 supplement to *Zbrano Delo*, or in Hartinger and Berger's *Ikarov sen*, and added to these a poem, 'When Spring Arrives', which we do not believe has been collected anywhere before. In each section there are further poems that might have been included. One particular regret is that there has not been the room to include any of the nine poems of the 'Tragedy of the Ocean', a sequence we have decided, ultimately, that it is better not to break up or excerpt.

As to the manner of presentation, we have attempted no typographical experimentation or variation other than that licensed by Kosovel's own manuscripts as reproduced in Berger/Hartinger, and in each of these cases have taken our lead, in translating these to the type-set page, from Ocvirk. One further advantage of Hartinger and Berger's reproduction of the manuscripts is that one can see not only the original forms and texts of the poems themselves, but the number of times they are accompanied by marginal notes and other forms of comment and supplementation by Kosovel. In several instances in this collection we have taken the liberty of reproducing these notes — even, in one case, in an instance where the note has been crossed out on the manuscript page — in the belief that this shows us, in a particularly direct manner, something which characterises Kosovel's poetry and may even be, in the Poundian sense, its *virtu*, namely its continual state of dynamic transition. In these annotated poems it is as if we are being given by Kosovel himself a particularly unambiguous indication that he finds the poem as he has as yet been able to develop it, as being in some manner still inadequate to the task he wishes it to perform, and so as in need of a kind of supplementation that, it may be, the style of the 'Kons' poems attempts to accomodate and the later poems integrate: a formal accompaniment, as it were, to that urge and belief we find presented in other poems, such as 'The Golden Boat' itself, as a necessary process, at once exhilarating and painful, of awakening and moving away from an earlier state of the self:

> I travelled in a golden boat
> over red evening waters
> among trees
> and grassy shores.
> I travelled,
> a golden sailor . . .
>
> But a storm blew up
> and the sun
> fell from its heights
> and as if everything else
> less golden, more clear,
> more vivid, shone,
> I stepped onto the shore
> revived.

Clearly, in poems like this, he is writing about the need to transcend, or to move into a new register, what has been seen as the deeply nostalgic self that had written the so-called 'Impressionist' poems of the Karst, but once we see this it becomes just as clear that those poems were themselves already transitional—that there is, at the very heart of them, an absence, a departure that has already happened, as if the boy who wrote them (for he was scarcely more than a boy) felt already the wind of the new century, tearing him away. For, very real wind as it most certainly is, the *burja* is also a powerful metaphor. The notorious sadness and melancholy which haunt so much of Kosovel's poetry—two more of his obsessive terms—become from this perspective the emotions of those numbed to—*by*—the wind of the new century, unable to see their way forward, or else, as betimes for Kosovel himself, those of someone who knows how much must be relinquished, put behind one, in order to become the new man, as Kosovel himself might put it, which that century is demanding. 'I am not sad', he says in 'Autumn Landscape', 'because I don't dwell on myself anymore'. 'To recognise yourself', he says elsewhere, 'look into the spherical mirror'—a convex mirror, surely, in which the self is foreshortened and so much more of the world is reflected.

Numerous people have supported these translations since the moment they heard about them. We would like to thank, in particular, John Kinsella, for introducing the proposal so enthusiastically to its publishers, and Aleksander Peršolja, who brought with him the support and resources of the Commune of Sežana, and the Slovenian Ministry of Culture.

DAVID BROOKS

.

# Part I
*The Golden Boat*

# Ballad

On a quiet autumn day
the juniper-bird
flies onto the Karst.

There is no-one
in the fields anymore,
only the bird
flying over the grass.
And only a hunter
watching her pass . . .

A shot in the silence;
a small spurt of blood;
and the juniper-bird
lies dead, lies dead.

# October

Wet gardens gleaming
in the evening gold. Brown barns, straw-
covered, darkening already.
In the evening wind the rain
rustles onto the ground.
It is sad and silent in the middle of the heart.

The fruits are picked, the trellises empty,
the last leaves still burning,
the swallows flown over the belfries,
one bird still singing in the distance.

All is silent, all dying
into the evening melancholy,
the fields darkening, my tightening heart
reflecting the green sky.

# A Premonition

Fields,
a ruined house by the road.
Darkness.
The silence of grief.

In the distance
a bright window.
Who?
A shadow against it.

Someone peers
after me;
with me
restlessness,
and a premonition
of death.

# Karst Village

I

Alone
through the village.
The vineyard trellises
howl in the darkness,
the *burja*
scales the walls, butts
the window: 'Who?'

The window
lightens the darkness.

At the end of the village
the pine-trees rustle,
tremble
when they recognise me.

II

Steep roofs sleep through the night,
straw roofs, stone roofs,
sombre
with lowered foreheads

people with arms crossed
over their chests.

How?
Why?
'You die, or you come back.'

III

A sea of pines
rustles darkly—
the Adriatic
butts at the shore,
into the darkness,
the *burja*
shaking a dead window.

It is night over the village on the Karst.

Who is despairing?
Who is moaning
that I may curse him
in my sick heart?

Who?

# Autumn

A light drizzle of rain.
The Karst roads are white.
The early morning is grey.

The pine is not stirring.
Where is this road hurrying to?
The early morning is grey.

The *brinovka* wakes,
shakes itself, and flies into the sky.
The early morning is grey.

# Dinner

A bowl of cooked, unpeeled potatoes.
Steam rising. A short prayer.
Then you take them out and eat.
Silence.
The family around.
On the wall a rosary
in father's memory.

The young man grabs his jacket
and goes into the village,
the others stay, praying.
The Karst.

## Last Night

Last night we listened to the *burja*
and didn't sleep at all;
we yarned quietly amongst ourselves
about strange and frightening things.

How it is on the sea
when ships sink
and how frightening and cold
and horrible the waves must be.

Last night we listened to the *burja*
and, truly, didn't sleep at all;
we wondered how nice it would be
to swim with the *burja* over the sea.

A cold morning dawned
(god knows where the ships were by then)
and in the orchard, from under the peach
and the apple trees, we picked up red fruit.

## Karst Autumn

The sweet red must, full clusters of grapes,
berries glistening in the rain.
In the distance the pine forest darkening,
poplars rustling below the mountain.

Autumn is coming, rustling in the lindens,
bending the poplars and the oak tree.
Some of us are in the cellar, some in the vineyard—
each in his fashion chasing sadness away.

# A Trip

Here and there. A fleeting departure.
A tree and a tower. And a house. Mountain. Hill.
Cold as sorrow. As silent dreams.
You are leaving. A dull and heavy throbbing.

A station. A restaurant. And leaves
falling across the tables from the chestnut trees.
And that lady. Quiet and alone.
A stare. Brown leaves. A fleeting impression.

Foreign land: like autumn and that stranger,
all fleeting, cold. But here with us warm.
Blowing leaves. Toward the Karavanke mountains.
A tunnel: in the semidarkness her shining eye.

———

This sad and golden autumn sun,
this freezing wind from the mountains, and us,
sitting and waiting for that train
which should come but never does.

# August

I love this quiet August rain
cooling the woods and the meadows,
this grey sky, this cold wind
coming into the heart's shadows.

It enters the calm heart quietly,
opening soundlessly to sorrow.
It is content at last in its sadness,
neither depressed nor exhausted now.

The grey, melancholy clouds are fragrant.
Everything has came to pass.
Through the rain, the wet, dark poplars
rustle in the fields of grass.

# Pines

Pines, pines, in silent horror,
pines in mute horror,
pines, pines, pines!

Dark pines
like sentinels below the mountain
across the stony paddocks
in a heavy, exhausted murmur.

When a suffering soul bends
on a clear night over the mountain
I can hear stifled voices
and can't sleep again.

'Weary, dreaming pines,
are my brothers dying,
is my mother dying
and my father calling me?'

Without answers they are rustling
as if in a weary nightmare,
as if my mother were dying,
as if my father were calling,
as if my brothers were suffering.

# Evening by the Red Sand Dune

A thick blue curtain of twilight
descends trembling from the sky;
for a moment the pines go quiet,
like a traveller stopping in the middle of a field.

Behind the hill the soundless village has darkened,
the steep roads have come to life again,
the gully by the sand-dune smells
of earth. The tower on the hill is silent.

Dark outlines, dull footsteps,
reapers crossing the muddy road,
heavy cattle drinking at the pond,
turning their heads at the hollow tread.

The poplars rustle, bending their crowns,
a star glimmers from the grey canvas overhead;
reapers' footsteps, cattle, all fade into darkness,
the moon appears from behind a thick cloud.

The whole of the Karst is soft—as if sobbing—
light drifts from the chapel, and organ sounds;
for a moment—and, like a rugged face,
the rocky desert falls silent in the moonlight.

## At a Provincial Station

On the brass (golden wheels
cogged and smooth, bony keys)
the sun glitters
as in semiclosed eyes.

Now and then a wheel starts up—
a distant chord waking;
the clerk unties the ribbon—
each day, a similar call . . .

Monotonous steps, locked into
the smell of the office—two rails into the world;
through the window—the Karst wilderness,
pines and juniper, acacia, wildflowers—
four trains a day.—

The bell rings;
he lifts his face from his fists
and starts up from sad dreams.

## All These Words

All these words should be
as fragrant as the sea of pines,
as morning stars
fading at dawn above the mountains . . .

But it is still midnight, midnight,
and I have to light them
so that we can stay
in this grey house on the Karst.

Wrapped in a black coat, I am saying them
into the *burja* as it hammers
on the windows; as my mother wakes,
thinks for a moment, and drifts into dream again . . .

But I am as wild as the *burja*—
and my sleep is long gone.
Silently I walk down the Karst roads.
The night is lighting my path.

# Night

The pines whispering, the waterfall murmuring,
the rocks like travellers, wrapped in grey coats,
stopped in the middle of the way,
the field like a trodden path
and the village like a bunch of children.
Everything silent.

But there, above the sea,
thousands of lights shining,
and there, by the shore,
a man who has sold his heart,
empty and hollow,
sobbing for this solitude.

# I Saw the Pines Grow

I saw the pines grow
into the sky. Calm stoics
through the flaring sun.
I saw a fire once
that would burn them up.

Like old men, the hills
leaned their heads onto their white pillows
and kept silent.
The pines are rustling.
(Who are they talking to?)

I saw how they wandered,
like burning pillars,
into the sky . . .

My body has collapsed into ashes.

## Cyclamens

Cyclamens
smell
as they did before.
The silver glow
of the moon
flows
into the valley.
Below the white windows
everything is quiet.
The moon
follows the silver road.

Cyclamens
smell
alone
alone
alone

## On the Park Bench

From the bench under the chestnuts
we stared as they walked past,
their figure full of springtime scents
and our smile was bitter.

They moved like slender vine-canes,
their bodies gently undulating,
as if behind rose curtains
their breasts were trembling.

They went with downcast eyes
and their look was hiding something,
but you could feel those hidden forces,
that passion you'd like to get drunk on.

# I Remember

I remember when I returned
and kept silent as the road
that sees everything but doesn't judge.

There, below that dark wall
I was taking leave of you,
kissing you so diffidently
on your sad, devoted eyes
and over your dark hair
and I held back gentle words
to be more like the Karst.

And as I was going home
I wept in the roadway
silently, so that the fields wouldn't hear,
silently, so that the plain wouldn't hear,
so that the trees wouldn't sob,
in the middle of the plain, silently, alone.

## My Mother Waits

Stranger, do you see that light burning in the window?
My mother is waiting for me, but I'm not coming,
everything is quiet in the night, the field is dark,
I wish I could go there now and kneel in front of her.

Mother, look: I don't want anything more from the world,
say a word, a word from your heart,
a word with a silent glow in it, a warm glimmer
for me wandering around exhausted, beaten.

See? She has extinguished the lamp. Why, I don't know.
I would go and look, stranger, but I'm not allowed.
Let me die here, now. See? My last glow,
my only one, has gone.

# In the Coffee Bar

I am thinking of you, my friend, sitting perhaps
in a suburban coffee bar, gazing in front of you;
the lamplighter goes down the street and lights the lamps,
quietly each of them flickers, and quietly burns . . .

The waiter is half asleep. And you too are silent,
wondering perhaps why you live, and burn;
outside the window (isn't it like an open eye?) lights are shining.
The thought stops. How many of them? One, two, three . . .

And already the thought wanders off: what, why, how;
isn't it just the same, whether three or three hundred?
The dark falls on the chairs, the tables, the billiard-corner;
isn't it the same, if there are a hundred of us or just two?
Hey waiter, can't you see? the bar is getting dark!
He wakes up, too (as from distant, perished dreams),
    and lights the lamps. . . .

# New Year Sonnet

Empty compartments . . . A light glimmers
and flickers through the hollow rumbling,
the silent, lonely fields extending;
it is hard for anyone who travels at this hour . . .

The conductor stares, leaning against the window,
losing his eyes on the darkened plain;
the heart would stop, the train is speeding,
it is hard for anyone who travels at this hour . . .

The heart would stop and dive
into the quiet silence of the dark valleys,
the heart would stop and hide
from the horror rising from memory;
in the house on the field a girl would
put out the light, for fear of unknown distances.

## Village Behind the Pines

Clutched in a hand of green pine,
a white, dusty village,
a half-sleeping village
like a bird in the nest of a hand.

I stop amidst the scent of the pines:
isn't this my own hand's hold?
A wide hold, a generous arch
for such a small group of children.

Someone is buried behind the church wall.
A dog-rose blooms on his grave.
From the white village, white roads
and every road leads to my heart.

# The Sun, Nada

The sun,
Nada, has set already,
as if hiding
from my eyes.
The sun
has sunk beyond the grove
and all is silent in the wood.
All? I don't know!
It's just that the shadows stare
mournfully,
the flowers breathe out their fragrance
in the dusk.
You can feel the tulips bleeding.
I could weep but I am not allowed.

# Just One Dread

There is just one dread — to be
in the midst of chaos, in the middle of the night,
searching for an exit, and feeling
there is no rescue, none.

Sometimes the golden glow of dawn
spills silently over the wounded rocks:
you want to go further
but you feel so worn

as if the dawn
hurts itself when it spreads its veil
and spills its burning fountain,
and calls to you from under the mountain:
Wake up! Look! The wounded range is blazing!
You feel it, but you don't believe in it.

―――

The wounded cascade that fell over
the sharp ridges of the mountain
has torn its golden veil.

# Death Sonnet

And all is nothing. These velvet eyes
are like sadness staring into grey,
their dark glow penetrating silence
like a sound getting lost in noise.

These silent, black, velvet eyes
with their dark reflection and grace
are kissing this grey sorrow
which smothers my soul more each day.

These silent, black, velvet eyes
are like the black, velvet sky
spread over the sharp wound of the Karst,
are like a lamp that calms the soul;
when it burns out over the broken land
the soul sinks into the soft darkness.

# Nocturne

I am hammering at my white Karst.
I am hammering at it in pain
thinking of Beethoven's face.

I am a pianist with iron hands.
The Karst is breaking, the earth bleeding,
but dawn is not coming.

Why are these white ships in the port?
The sailor has hidden his face behind a yellow sail.
(The sun is burning.) What is his dream?

I understand.
A quiet insurrection is taking shape.
With burning tentacles it is conquering souls.

Are you in the middle of a road?
Start again from scratch.
Cleanse yourself in the fire. Become our brother!

# My Poem

My poem is an explosion,
a wild raggedness. Disharmony.
My poem doesn't want to reach you
who by divine providence, divine will
are dead aesthetes, museum moths,
my poem is my face.

# The Ninth Country

The bells toll midday from the churches of Ljubljana.
I walk down the road to lunch
like everyone else who doesn't know where to go,
grateful at least of that one goal.

I walk. My vulgar laugh
flies into everyone's face.
A gentleman shaking his head, adjusting his dress-coat.
My laugh wants the truth.

Those who were overturning the world
have by now sobered up
and those who did not do any overturning,
remain as vulgar as they were before.

And it is so dull, dull and tedious.
The idea of revolutions has died out.
The procession goes on (a man nailed to the cross!)
and behind it a line of abbots.

# This Horrible Time

This horrible, unsettling time
is flooding our search with disquietude—
in every direction, every direction,
breaking and killing our dreams.
Crime—Sacrament, the sacrament is a crime,
suffering attached to love,
the heart's cold temples plundered
as if they were damned.
From dead and abandoned dwellings
grey, desperate prayers are sailing—
European man, half-dead,
calling for salvation . . .

## On a Grey Morning

On a grey morning
I walk the streets downtown,
the fog cuts into my burning eyes,
it cuts into my throat,
and is cold around my heart.

Then, from the bakeries,
the smell of fresh rye bread,
but the bakeries are still dark,
the street silent, nobody yet around
and I feel tight in my soul.

It is the memory of the Karst:
a village strewn among the rocks
that this black bread reminds me of,
this healthy scent from the bakeries
that smells so much like a caress.

# Melancholy of Hunger

Hunger bites from the hard wall,
a human is not a human any more.
Grey stone is your comrade,
cold,
grey
stone.

Pour, pour, cold rain,
cold autumn rain,
pour, pour silent rain,
pour over the graves.

# The Golden Boat

I travelled in a golden boat
over red evening waters
among trees
and grassy shores.
I travelled,
a golden sailor . . .

But a storm blew up
and the sun
fell from its heights
and as if everything else
less golden, more clear,
more vivid, shone,
I stepped onto the shore
revived.

Red clouds
tore from my heart,
I saw them
and followed them
through the world.

# Ecstasy of Death

All is ecstasy, the ecstasy of death!
The golden towers of Western Europe,
white domes—(all is ecstasy!)—
all is drowning in the burning, red sea,
the sun sets and gets drunk in it,
the thousand-times-dead European.
—All is ecstasy, the ecstasy of death.—

The death of Europe will be beautiful, beautiful,
like a luxuriant queen dressed in gold
she will lie in a coffin of dark centuries,
and die silently, as if she were
closing, ancient, her golden eyes.
—All is ecstasy, the ecstasy of death.—

From the evening cloud (the last
messenger to bring Europe light!)
blood spills into my tired heart,
and o, there is no water left in Europe
and we people drink blood,
blood from the sweet evening clouds.
—All is ecstasy, the ecstasy of death.—

Just born, and already you burn in the fire of evening,
all seas are red, all seas
full of blood, all lakes, and no water,
no water for this human to wash his guilt,

to wash his human heart,
no water to quench his thirst
for the quiet, green morning land.

All is evening and morning won't come
until we all die who carry the guilt of dying,
until we all die
to the last.

Ay, into this landscape, even this green,
dewy landscape, even into this
you will shine, evening sun,
with burning rays? Even into this?

The sea is flooding the green plains
the sea of stinging evening blood
and there is no salvation, none
until we both fall, you and I,
until we fall, I and all of us,
until we all die under the weight of blood

the sun will shine on us,
European corpses,
with golden rays.

# A Sketch at the Concert

The black piano is full of dreams
as if the depth of twilight
were reflected in it.

Behind it, the pianist
has spread his white hands.

Quietly
as if over a black
marble lake
two white swans have swum away
to search for the infinite . . .

## As If they were Landscapes

As if they were landscapes, quiet and marvellous,
the most secret thoughts hiding amidst them,
I live in them, staring as they flow
like one valley into another.

As if I were parting sea-shores with my hand
I find, always, new worlds beyond them
and to my eyes it seems
I am wandering further and further away.

As I part them further and wider
I grow like a tree from a shining mosaic
into an invisible tree
at the heart of the world.

And what's left to me, at the end of this growing?
I have found all these landscapes, far and unknown,
but when I close my eyes
my soul seeks new growth still . . .

## Astral Erotics

Miriam, the name
has a scent of lilies under the moon
in the dark, hidden shadows of the garden
from where my memories come.

I know you are disturbed by my rhymes
and avoid them like enemies,
but, my friends, without rhymes
you will miss all harmonies.

Behind the bushes, the trees, the silent plain,
runs the river with its green surface
sleeping under the moonshine,
drinking in the night's silence.

## The Gathering

God knows
what our silent, exhausted faces are dreaming.
Outside the storm is shaking the trees.
Each one of us is alone.

A cold, rustling September rain
falls over the dark fields.
In the quiet of the room the warm light
soothes the divided heart.

We are brothers, strangers,
each one hiding his own defeats,
the silent evening wrapping our hearts
in a gossamer of sorrowful dreams.

## People with a Wound

People with a wound,
with a wound in their heart,
hide it
with their palm
but see: it's as if their palm
were as translucent as the white leaf
of a lily
with a red
heartbeat,
as if the wound
was the wound of the whole world.—
You want to hide it,
but everybody recognizes it.

## I Am

I am, and I'm not asking why;
my word is that I am here,
silently growing into this silent place
as if I were growing from peace.

Beyond the huts, the fields, beyond the gardens,
as if dreams were shining on them,
behind the narrow paths, the fences,
across the meadows stretches a restful silence.

I am, and I am not asking why,
with the huts, the fields, the gardens,
this place is like a sleeping lake
untroubled by waves.

## There is No Death

There is no death, no death!
It's only that the silence is too deep.
Like in a green
wide forrest.

Only that you fade,
only that you become silent,
only that you become lonely,
alone and unseen.

Oh, there is no death, no death!
It's only that you fall,
you fall,
in an abyss of infinite blue.

## The White House

The white house
stares into the green field
and you stare with it.—

When you gaze like that
through the transparent window
doesn't it seem
the towers of eternity are everywhere?

This tree
that sprang up
straight as an arrow from the ground,
this grey rock, like a pilgrim
come to a sudden halt.—

The simpler these
grey faces are
the more they are full
of a sacred mystery.

If I don't save them
darkness will colour them
with miraculous mosaics;
if I don't save them
then you, sorrow,
will redeem me with a kiss!

## I Am Not Alone

The man on a bicycle
riding down the autumn road
is still with me.
There's an umbrella in my room.
The sun is shining
on the white pages,
burning with white flame
like I do.

My heart cannot call you back again.
The sun is shining on the young corpses,
abandoning this place,
and I see that all is still with me.
The yellow leaves
followed you
but have fallen back
on the Karst.

## The Sail

Amidst the grey of sulphuric waters
it has swayed since the beginning of history,
each wave has already reached its shore
but the sail can't leave the middle of the sea.

In a sickly stupor it must plunge and ascend,
everything whirling into its sway,
everything, like tormenting and weary dreams,
there is no end to the horror, no end.

On the side of the boat the mute
deathless sailors lean,
their eyes searing flames
they have long since wanted to put out.

But the eyes stare and stare
to catch the dawn;
o, this primeval, primordial quest—
herds of fog hurry over the sea.

If it were the heart, it would become speechless,
if it were the soul, it would wear out,
if dreams, the fog would cover them,
if tears, they would turn to stone.

# Part II
*Integrals*

# Rhymes

Rhymes have lost their value.
Rhymes aren't convincing.
Did you hear the traction of the wheels?
The poem should be the traction of pain.

What's the point of phrases, dear orator?
Store phrases in museums.
Your words need traction
to grab a man by the heart.

Everything has lost its value.
The white sea of the spring night
is washing through the fields and gardens.
A presentiment of the future is passing us by.

# Autumn Quiet

It is quiet as autumn inside me
and outside. Beautiful
as far as I can think.

A big job awaits me.
Isn't that joyful?

I am not striving
for an honorary award
in the society of man,
just for
a world of beauty
and justice.

What is joy?
The wish to live
The joy of life.
Who cares for awards!

I am a step closer to life
in which I must make
my mark.

———

Pseudocultural institutions,
an indifferent public, unclear cults, struggle
for Slovenism. [Crossed out in manuscript]

# Kons: The Cat

The cat jumped through the window.
Jumped onto the piano.
Played, and wondered:
When I jump, the piano sings.
I was in the next room
and thought that a ghost was playing.
But it struck once more
and the cat jumped
through the window.

Everywhere a new poet walks
the piano responds.
But unlike the cats
nothing disturbs him.

The whole world is captivated:
this man
is a fool.
But a poet.
*And all listen to his steps*
singing as if on a
piano.

# Evacuation of Spirit

Spirit in space.
A blaze of storms ignites the dark.
Spirit burns in space.
A dispersal of magic lights.
Green windows of an illuminated
express on the viaduct.
I am burning and lighting my own way.
The blind only feel the electricity
of my light, they don't see its glow,
but they all shudder, like I do,
as if dying from poison;
they don't realize that this is the quivering
of the wings wanting to unfurl,
to burn like a golden fire into the night.
They curse the sun's police
because they sleep at night
like suburban gents.

But all people sleep at night
without the magic revelations
shining in me and out of me.
People are an evacuation of spirit,
a psychological anomaly.

# Kons: ABC

Stay cold, heart!
A cynic.
A transformer.
The Orient Express on the Paris viaduct.
Arms in chains.
Cars run.
I can't.
My thought-electricity
is in Paris.
The smell of medicine
from the clinics.
*Shame*—
(Spit. Be scornful.)—
*Shame, Shame,*
*Shame!*

## Prostituted Culture

Tired elders selling themselves,
being what they didn't want to be.
I despair three times a day
and curse myself
and the universe.
Napoleon goes to Russia.
Look how these
red autumn roses fade.
Are you a madman or what,
weeping with the leaves in the wind?
This is your true face
pure as the autumn sun
reflected in tearful eyes.
(The tears are like gold!)
He, the Black King, wants
a double face.
Tomorrow: leave for Paris.

# The Mystic Light of Theory

The mystic light of theory.
I live in misery.
A notion of solar energy.
An ox observes itself in the pond
but does not understand its image.
*Association?*
Politics is dying.
The rest mourning.
Quick lime.

**1**

A black train goes under the mountain
like a mole.
A grey face at a grey window.
Through the window leans a lady
with glacé gloves.
The statics of sadness: melancholy.
The country.

World events and
REVOLUTIONS
KINGS
ARTISTS

But here only thatch.
Someone down the road
whistling a mournful march.
March, man, out of this unjust country!
Like the fat butcher's lady
the fat sun
is strolling through the village.
The sun is mournful.

## My Black Inkpot

My black inkpot is taking a walk.
In a tuxedo.
Like the fog.
The whole country veiled, deaf.
A melancholy cat lies in the hay.
Whining on its golden violin!
Yea, yea, yea.

**A A A**

**A A A**

# Kons. 5

Dung is gold
and gold is dung.
Both = O
O = ∞
∞ = O
AB<
1, 2, 3.
Whoever has no soul
doesn't need gold.
Whoever has a soul
doesn't need dung.
EE-AW

# Integrals

A rotational evening.
Trees by green water.
Rotation of the spirit.
My spirit is red.

I love my pain
I work from pain.
Even more, even more:
from the bottom of my consciousness.

From the bottom of my consciousness
so that everything is in vain.
Profiteers
dance the can-can.

## Above the Madhouse

A lunatic moon
is strolling above the madhouse.
Across the white garden
a shadow is walking—a man
pondering his own sad beard.
As if in a kaleidoscope
currencies and shares
are dancing in front of him
burning in a rainbow fire.
Once a banker, a prisoner of papers,
he now strolls
with the lunatic moon
behind the white walls of the madhouse.

This is that
horrible freedom
when you step behind the invisible walls
of the expanded human consciousness
and diverge into a terrible
immensity.

## Objects Without Soul

A cupboard with red glass panes.
Boredom sleeping in the corner.
The automobile is a sensation.
The cosmic breath: an earthquake.

On the bright dawn:
A red ATOM
My unwritten word
reflection
reflection
The laugh of king Dada
on a wooden horse
Ho, Ho,
Hum.

# The Laugh of King Dada

Order No. 35:
Suddenly it's become apparent
that the red sunset
is dangerous to the state.
Therefore every time
the sunset appears
it has to be jailed
in the black sea.
On the gold mosaic of a tomb
the glittering red sunset
is shining.
A lonely horse is strolling
over the fields.
The magic of sunset!
The horse is melancholic.

———

King DADA
has insured himself against death
at the ABC
King DADA is afraid
of assassins.

## A Heart in Alcohol

Lift the veil of melancholy!
Your future's in laughter.
The sun is shining behind the dark glass.
The plain is golden with the sun.
There is sadness in your golden eyes.
Don't look at yourself in the mirror!

Laughter, laughter, laughter.
Snow clouds.
In the spring blue.　　　　DEATH
Space O ∞ O　　　　　　SWIMMING
the etherial　　　　　　IN THE ETHER
The train is as slow as a black snail.
Thought is like lightning.
Under the grey wall of Triglav
we are resting.
Our thoughts: beyond.

## Poem No. X

Poison for the rats. *Pif!*
*Pif, Pif, Pif, Kh.*
*KH. KH. KH.*
A rat is dying in the attic.
Strychnine.

Ah, my young days,
like quiet sun in the attic.
Above the roof I smell
the scent of linden trees.

Die, Die, Die, Die
Die
Human
Human
Human.
At 8.00 there's a lecture
on human ideals
The newspapers are bringing pictures
of the Bulgarian hangings.
People?
They read and fear God.
God, though, is busy.

# The Spherical Mirror

Is it the mirror's fault
you've got a hooked nose?
Glory be to Heine!
To recognize yourself
look into the spherical mirror.
Nationalism is a lie.
Chestnuts rustle beside the water,
autumn has come to the secondhand dealers.
Their shops are full of antiques.
*Cin, cin.*
Give up on yourself.
A red chrysanthemum.
An autumn tomb . . .
a white tomb.
Ivan Cankar.

THE GOLDEN BOAT

WHY DID YOU LET

INTO THE MARSHES?

# Kons

The tiger jumped onto the tamer
and tore him to pieces.
You can't train a beast,
There is no training nature.
You can't mechanize people.
There is no culture in mechanics.

Learn from this example:
Karel Čapek R.U.R.
Man burst from the homunculus
a thousand times more horrible.
Harmony is goodness.
Step down from the stage, idiot.
Man: this is a new word.
Destroy the Taylorians
FACTORIES    THE HOUSE
DESTROY    OF BRICKS
Man is not an automaton.

# Kons: XY

A big elephant is walking through my heart.
Kludsky Circus: Entry 5 Din.
Don't make a song and dance about it.
She is smiling: *cin, cin.*

Peoples' hearts are small and prisons are large,
I would like to walk through people's hearts.
Do you follow this or that clique?
A thousand dinars or jail for 7 days.

The roses in my heart never weep.
Who could be young and yet depressed?
What if a cop were coming through the door?
A military trial, you'd be thrown into jail.

Roses, keep to yourself these difficult days.
Cop, your eyes are like a bayonet,
stupid and evil. (Roses, close your eyes!).
Gandhi's been locked up for a whole six years.

# Kludsky Circus, Seat 461

Circus.
Gallery.
Seat No. . . .
Colombine
undresses, undresses.
Everybody watches.
Nobody sees
that she is hanging by her teeth.
Rising. Already near the tent-top.
Insolent comments.
Shameful laughter.
Now she sheds her last veil.
They watch her,
biting with their eyes
into her soft body.
They applaud.
She has beautiful thighs.
Wavy breasts.
They applaud
and mock
her suffering
and insult her.

See, the animal
is applauding the human.
The human is animal.
The animal is human.
The valve bursts.
The lions are raging.

# Poem No. 1

The sun is shining.
I wake up
I'm still thinking about the circus
and Colombine.

The sunshine is on the road.
The sunshine is going with me.
At the tobacconist
I buy four Zetas.
O, how small
the tobacconist is
compared to the sun.
Man is like a little lizard
that likes the sun.
And yet
the sunshine is following me!

## Conversation at Twilight

Our windows are netted.
White barricades.
The Indians
don't know a thing
about gravitation.
But the dynamite explodes also
on Novaya Zemlja.
A gentleman with an astrakhan hat!
There is no arithmetic centre
between the old and new worlds.
A person can be young or old.
A golden boat on the horizon.
Natural laws = Ethics???
You can understand the universe
even without physics.

The hanged men
swing from the telegraph poles.
Admission: one dinar.
It rains.
You talk with the universe.
A barn in front of the window.

# Kons: 4

Boston is accusing Einstein
Einstein is banned.
Relativity dangerous?
In Berlin
they are locking up
Chinese students.
Chinese students dangerous?
The SHS is changing the government.
It has changed many governments already.
France. Spain. Morocco.
The corporal terrorizes.
The cop terrorizes.
Big people live
according to their souls' desires,
small people by the letter of the law.
§ x: 14 days in jail.
§ y: To the gallows.
§ z: Into exile.
I have been locked up 21 years.
10 times on the gallows
I am exiled forever.
Hey, darling, want to cry?
I am not able to cry.
I am as hard as a blade
that has to stab the heart.

## Grey

My heart is
grey from the streets,
grey from stone.
**THE DEAD FOOTSTEPS OF PRISONERS
ARE BEATING INTO IT.**
**Do you want to be happy?**
**Don't wish for happiness.**

D Y N A M I S M
ACTIVITY **B**
BALKANS

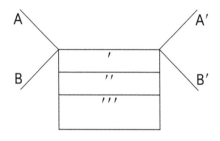

'   expressionism of life
''   vacuum, economic,
    political depression, etc
'''   The foundation of the
    future

AA' — depression
BB' — action
≡ **real work**

Fernando, scourge of Asturia

## Lord Radić

Lord Radić is selling hats.
Better to sell hats than men.
Black horses on the white snow
are fleeing, fleeing, fleeing, where to?
I would like to be alone.
To flee into the fields
and in the midst of the snow
in the white silence of the heart
to fall asleep, fall asleep.

———

To die.
The red chimney whistles.
*Too, too, too.*
*Loo, loo, loo*
There is no peace.

# Hey, Hey

Hey hey, it's raining over the grey houses of Ljubljana
wrapping them in a grey curtain against the sun.
In Trieste they are burning our *Edinost*.
Christ has come into the League of Nations.
No, not that good, beautiful Christ, glowing with the glory of love.
A pseudo Christ is in Geneva.
What, is it raining in Geneva too?
Christ has come among the brown insurgents
and is standing there on the grey street
chasing away the scribes and pharisees.
He is shooting and killing,
shooting and killing.
O you nation of sheep, you white nation,
now do you understand what you are?

# Near Midnight

Near midnight,
flies dying in the cup,
the fire gone out.
Beautiful Vida
a bitter memory.
Stravinsky in a car.
The roaring of the sea.
O to be alone for five minutes!
The heart—Trieste—is ill.
That is why Trieste is beautiful.
Pain flowers in beauty.

## Kons. Kons. Kons.

Moonlight as cold as icecream,
empty as the songs of the troubadours.
It is nice to be sitting in the shade of night.
Latrines. Pissoirs. Here.
A man behind the door. What does he want?
He stands there like a shade
behind the transparent doors
of moonlight.
Moonlight over the fields
like a petrified illness . . .
Your body
glimmers in the moonlight.

# Delirium

A martyrdom of thoughts.
Blue sea.
Grey prison.
A soldier is impaling
hopeless thoughts
on his bayonet
in front of the window

Pardon me. 'O, nothing.'
*Sigaretta.*
*Eine Edison.*
I hear the blue sea
butting monotonously
into my skull

# Cops

*Cops are people of the lowest quality.*
Servants at their owners' commands.
I am a stranger to the green field.
Shrewd as a snake, humble as a dove.
To live. All who are persecuted want to live.
*To live with dignity.*
The sun hangs in the tower
THE GREEN PARLIAMENT
**OF FROGS**
I live in a country
of European wildcats.
Symmetry is beautiful.
*The political crooks are free!*

## At the Station

A carriage. An open door.
And a fence.
A man
pacing the platform.
A red cap.
A red flag
stopping the train.
*In the square of the door*
*a man.*
A fence.
A green clearing.
Someone departing.
O man with a heart
you'd better not!
Once more
I look back.
In the silver distance
smoke.

# The Longhaired Romantic

At a sad window.
Each departure
is only for once.
I hear the blue horse.
Is he coming with you,
longhaired romantic?
Poplars beside autumn roads.
Where are the poets, that they
don't notice these poplars?
A white cemetery wall.
Romantics.

At a sad window.
She leans over the carnations.
The sun is shining
into her black tearful eyes.

## A Sign Above the Town

Cars 4 km, thoughts 1 km,
anticipation 100m.
Stupidity Zone: the idiot stares,
the donkey rules, the poet moans
for the moonlight—hey, got an enema?

Hello! Physics! This isn't the Balkans.
An order for soap. Sun in the chestnuts.
I laugh at the black-eyed girl
in love with me. The nymph
has married. I'll go there, a miserable poet.

Across the black lake with oars:
*clap—clap—clap—clap*
my little boat *aslap*
to where she sits in front of the castle
and waits for me.
Dogs must be on a leash, otherwise there's a fine.

# KONS

A tired European
stares sadly into a golden evening
even sadder
than his soul.
The Karst.
A civilization without heart.
A heart without civilization.
An exhausting struggle.
An evacuation of souls.
The evening scorches like fire.
Death of Europe!
Mercy! Mercy!
Herr professor,
do you understand life?

# Ljubljana is Sleeping

In the red chaos
the new humanity is coming! Ljubljana is sleeping.
Europe is dying in a red light.
All telephones have been cut.
O, but there's the cordless one!
A blind horse.
[Your eyes are like those
in Italian paintings.]
White towers are rising from brown walls.
A deluge.
Europe is stepping into a tomb.
We are coming with the hurricane.
With poisonous gases.
[Your lips are like strawberries.]
Ljubljana is sleeping.
The tram conductor is sleeping.
In the Europa Cafe they are reading
the *Slovenian Nation.*
A rattle of billiard balls.

# Herrings

A barrel of herrings
arrived in Ljubljana.
They were asked
about their political persuasion.

They said
they were from Iceland.
Modern poets
warn of decay.
The herrings
had been sealed all week in the barrel
and they stank.

## Black Walls

Black walls are breaking
over my soul.
People are like
falling, extinguishing lanterns.

A one-eyed fish
swims in the darkness,
black-eyed.

Man comes
from the heart of darkness.

## Our Eyes

Our eyes were flooded
by burning lava
and the grey dust
of cement towers
seared our lips.

Like burning trees
we bent
into the new day.

## Europe is Dying

Europe is dying.
The League of nations and the pharmacy
each is a lie.
Operations. Revolutions!
I am standing on a grey road.
Brown leaves are falling from the trees.
There is only one thing I fear:
that when these trees are black and bare
and the fields
and small houses are grey,
and I scream,
everything, everything around
will be silent.

## A Reflection from the Attic
*or, the mystery of space*

In semi-darkness
there's a blackened staircase.
Doors
Doors
Doors
Through the open attic
comes the silver light
of a storm.
On the wall a mystically
bright reflection.
I lie on the stairs
and my shadow
is drawn into the silver reflection
as if into a silver mirror.

# Impression

The *burja* has opened the window.
Warm stars
are falling over the fields.
Spring.
Spring.

A white face has beamed
in the azure,
silk rustled
in the valley.

A glassy sky
has broken,
above us soft, dark clouds.
Silk.

## A Bottle in a Corner

They are building a house.
A bottle in a corner
tells more
than a collection of empty rhymes.
Stereotypical naturalism.
Realism smells
of mortar.
On the veranda
I look over green
fields.

The clouds over the fields
are grey
like a November
cemetery.

# Poem

I sit and write.
By my window
golden fruit.
Everything is a poem.
On my window
there are no white curtains.

Even these red leaves
on the trellis: a poem.
A tiger-striped cat
watches me.
Her eye: a camera obscura.
Green secret.

I am thinking of you, leaving
like a white swan
across red water.

# Kons

An angry autumn is coming.
The stars are cynical.
One, two, three, four, five,
everyone damned
all of us
one, two, three.
A white fence,
a shadowy villa.
You have drawn
a dewy curtain.

My thought
is brighter than a star.
I wander without a purpose
and your dog
barks at me.

## *The Devil*, You'd Say

*The devil*, you'd say
and order another jug of wine.
Didn't the artistic heart
die at 4 pm?
The sound of the bells is hollow. Those are
empty songs. I know them.

I like only one of them.
The requiem, which nobody has
damaged yet.

For quite a while I've lived
on poison and hate, contempt and laughter,
and pain
is my only consolation.
Ah, but I smile at these idiots.
You, with bloated faces!
Still: I live.

# The Red Rocket

I am a red rocket, I ignite
myself and burn and fade out.
    Yes, I in the red vestments!
    I with the red heart!
    I with the red blood!
    I am escaping tirelessly, as if
I alone must reach fulfilment.
    And the more I escape, the more I burn.
    And the more I burn, the more I suffer.
    And the more I suffer, the faster I fade out.
    O, I, who want to live forever. And
I go, a red man, over a green field;
above me, over the azure lake of silence,
clouds of iron, o, but I go,
I go, a red man!
    Everywhere is silence: in the fields, in the sky,
in the clouds, I'm the only one escaping, burning
with my scalding fire and
I can't reach the silence.

# The Singing Arc Lamp

The night stands.
(An open window.)
Time passes by the window.
In the lamp
a mysterious voice is burning,
as if the emptiness
of centuries were alive.—
No one walks anymore
through the circle of light.

The footpath is empty.
The house,
only the night house keeps silent.

## A Face at the Window

I love you, grey face in the grey
café window, hopeful
face.
In a time of broken harpoons,
ships, masts—in the heart a quiver
of arrows—in the eyes a grey lethargy
you should know:
it spills over us
like a flood of light
from the sky.

We will be able to look upon
the green heaving of the seas
and see terrifying whirlpools,
sailors on the masts
without fear.

# A Streetlamp

What would you be, human, if it's hard
for you to be a human? Become a street-
lamp, quietly spreading
its light onto humans.
Let them be as they are, because as it is
they are always themselves with a human face.
Be good to them, these humans,
and impartial like the streetlamp
that silently lightens the drunkard's face
and vagrants and students
over the lonely road.

Be a streetlamp,
if you can't be a human
because it is hard to be a human.
A human has only two hands
but should help thousands.
So be a streetlamp
that lights a thousand happy faces,
that lights the lonely, the wanderer.
Be a lamp with a single bulb,
a person in a magic square
signalling with a green hand.
Be a lamp, a lamp,
a lamp.

# Autumn

A green wreath freezes
on the grave of a friend.
A burglary at midnight.
The workshop—a temple.
When does the express leave for Ljubljana?
The silver smoke winds itself
amongst blue mountains.
Art is a progressive
cultural factor!
Cold is descending into my heart.
Aeroplanes expand the horizon,
they lift the cosmic consciousness.
Love awakens the spirit.
The psychology of consciousness.
The spirit, the soul, reason.
The modern lyric is in decline.
At 2000 metres in the air
there is no more perspective.

An autumn storm over the sea.
Through point zero
into red chaos.
A cosmic experience:
if you walk along a silver autumn road
you can experience the cosmic feeling.
Black forests.
The century is mechanised.
The sky is not mystic
but **SPACE**.
In the attic I have hunger for a friend,
the bitter bread of life.
Autumn from a white balcony.
Genius = spirit + reason.
A dark, cold autumn night.
Autumn wind.

Dynamists.
The air is cold from the rain
and September moonlight
on the Karst, mysterious.

## In Green India

In green India among silent
trees bending over blue water
lives Tagore.

Time there is captured in an azure circle,
the clock does not tell the month or year
but spreads quietly
as if from invisible centres,
over trees and mountains, over the ridges of temples.

There nobody is dying, nobody is bidding farewell;
life is like eternity, caught in a tree.

# Kaleidoscope

The kaleidoscope of the macrocosm
is the microcosm.
Glistening dew.
Fragrant eyes.
Is the grass green?
Man is white.
Movement. Music.
Type expands into space.
Voices are like buildings.
A draught of winds.
Cosmos, cosmos, cosmos.
Magic of space.
Glimmering of space.
The light of the soul
shines through the poem,
the light of the word,
like rainbow glass.
Don't wake the corpse!
Biology = a spiritual science,
Geography = a science of humankind,
Politics = a science of reason.
Heart, heart, heart.
Constructivity sees
cosmos in the object.
A human is an object with a soul and a body.
Are you uncomfortable in 3rd class?
There are young ladies in the compartment.
We are travelling into the cosmos.

I am stepping through type —
behind the golden curtain.
Through golden type.
A revolution of angels.
Hey, hey, hey?

# A Suicide in Front of a Mirror

A suicide in front of the mirror.
A frightened soul.
A wind moaning in the black woods.
A night storm tearing the heart from my chest.

You, my spirit, Flying Dutchman,
always returning to the primal dark
getting drunk on the storm's blowing.
In the street a policeman's at work.

It is awful to be brother to the storm!
Awful to be brother to the silver sun.
Stay, spirit, broken and weary,
don't seek a solution from the black shores.

I walk through the forest. The trunks are black.
Two are leaning on each other.
Above me the black chasm of the universe.
I am leaning into it, listening.

# Sketch

By my bed
there's a gun.
During the night
when I'm ill
and wake from a dream
I open the window and shoot into the dark
(a calm wave of silent azure
carries the stars
gently beyond the mountains)
because I feel anxious:
around me corpses are glowing,
all of them my brothers,
my young eyeless brothers!

I shoot for help
because it seems to me
that everything around me is burning,
around them, whom I love.

My brother brings me
clear water—I can see them
even more distinctly now.

And then the night again
and the heavy sweating.

## Blue Horses

Blue horses go over the fields.
They are cloaked in moonlight.
You? You are here?
A graveyard of dreams.
A city lies there
incinerated.
Bright dawn breaking over it.
It is nice to be dead.
HP75.

# Autumn Landscape

The sun is autumnally calm
as if it were mourning
behind the slender cypresses
behind the white cemetery wall.

The grass is all red in the sunshine.
Do you wear dogmatic shoes?
A bicycle alone on the autumn road.
You ride through a dying landscape.

A sober person walks over a field,
as cold as autumn
as sad as autumn.
Belief in humankind.
That is a sacred thought to me.
A speechless silence is like sadness.
I am not sad,
because I don't dwell on myself anymore.

# Part III

# When Spring Arrives

When Spring arrives, Elgie the sailor's daughter's
nights are full of cries into life;
whole nights she wanders among the stars
seeking lost landscapes.

They say that she is very strange,
that sometimes she shouts for joy, sometimes tiredly,
keeps silent and is dark as a mountain,
and that there is no room under her breasts for a heart.

Her brothers and sisters are thieves,
some are sailors going to distant places,
some are masons raising walls.
She swims in the golden waves of the sea
And flies like a butterfly in the wind.

# A Cold Thought

A cold thought
full of power
shivers in the silver night.

What are you aiming at?
Be quiet
as the winter lake.
Be still.
The silver energy
seeps through the veins of dark.

A silver flood
over the night roads.

# Bianca

She moved across the fields
as cool as the dawn
wrapped in a bright blue veil.

She moved across the sun
as if she were dreaming,
the veil fluttering in the wind

as if the dreams had recognised
the time to leave her dark eyes
and abandon the burning Karst

and her eyes were staring after them.
But I, a rock in the fields,
waited in vain for them to burst into flame.

# Green Parrot

Hey, green parrot!
Tell us how it is in Europe!
The Green parrot replies:
Man is not symmetrical.

# Autumn Day

I used to live in Trnovo;
an unpleasant room
with its window to the East—
grey morning across the roofs.
Morning, and sad, beautiful evenings,
but I have no window into the evening
when I think of the Karst.
On the Karst the leaves are turning red.
Grape harvest, etc. Me here.
Unhappy, I go from Trnovo into town.
The river Gradaščica rustles all green
carrying orange leaves;
children playing with a cat
while they load sand on heaps.
The kitten watches and thinks:
yes, little one, you
like me. (Is this the little cat
miaowing in the evening
climbing under my coat
in the cold nights
when I was coming home?
[The little child slept like an angel.])

The child—a sunny new world
Sun—child—kitten
autumn sun. Quiet.
Sun!
Sun!
And myself.

Something stirred in the alley.
I went towards the city.

Where do you feel the infinite,
immensity, beauty?

A child is like the ocean,
the sun is reflected in him.
A small world dwells in him,
but infinite.

A world of two or three images
but immense.
These images move and live.
Hey!

# In My Room

At night I lie in my room
with boxes and an empty desk
that I spend all my sad hours at
and the happy ones too, hours
that shine like a fire
over the night town.
In the night I wake up.
In the thick dark the flames
of my dark book of revelation
flare as if it wants to immolate itself,
flare, as if unable to live any longer.

Oh my unwritten book,
my book of burning insights,
flaring energies, dreams,
your letters blaze golden in the night
into someone who is sick like me,
and must go through death
into a new day.
The letters burn gold,
like a secret door, like a heavy fence
I step through
into a new landscape.

## Moon over the City

The moon over the city is departing.
The chestnut is motionless and silent.
Just one leaf quivering
in the night landscape.

Silver roofs, white towers,
all blush in the dawn,
just one leaf in shadow;
quiet over the gardens.

People have woken from their dreams,
each face radiant with joy;
only one is still at the window,
drunk with the loneliness of Spring.

## A Ship Departing

A ship is departing, its white breast
full of the heavy gold of evening,
a white wave rustles over the green sea
the golden glow of cathedrals

*amor inertus.*
Departure **Worldliness**
on a ship.

Yesterday I stood by the sea.

Avoid elaborate sentences
your face might drown in them.
~
Evening above the house. Like a volcano
where gold is on fire, and from the gold
a smoke of silver. Twilight sets, submerges.
The sun glows, glows.
~
I hate all the years
that passed by me into the world
while I stood bending over the ground,
three times five hundred years.

# Negative Total

Our life is like a road,
cut off, narrow, without horizon,
desire impaled in the chest,
a negative total.

~

The ideal of life. An Ode to Life
Philosophy—religion
The ultimate]—∞ eternity
*Math.* eternity
the unalterable
philos.—conception of the world

## Windelband.

Why is there a light in the middle of the village,
since it is impossible to live?

~

I am like a force between un-
dulating forces unable to find
equilibrium.

~

Autumn. Late moonlight.

# Italian Culture

The Slovenian National House in Trieste, 1920.
The Workers House in Trieste, 1920.
Wheat fields in Istria on fire.
Fascist threat during the elections.
The heart is becoming as tough as a rock.
Shall Slovenian workers' homes
continue to burn?
The old woman is dying at her prayers.

Slovenism is a Progressive Factor,
Humanism is a Progressive Factor
A humanistic Slovenism: synthesis of development.
Gandhi, Gandhi, Gandhi!
*Edinost* is burning, burning,
our nation, choking, choking.

# 3

The Slovenian poem is dying.
Its sorrow is a heavy wine.
Its home is a smoky tavern.
Outside life is singing.

The Slovenian poem is dying.
Poets with decaying hearts.
They smell of spilt wine,
all the poems stink of smoke.

Outside the scent of the graceful linden trees,
cars—a joyful life.

A Slovenian poet should have
a heart as clear as an azure crystal,
a heart as healthy as linden flowers,
a heart as healthy as rosemary.

The Slovenian poem is dying
from the heavy intoxication of the wine.
Along the white road amongst the linden trees
a red car is passing.

## The Syphilitic Captain

The syphilitic captain
ordered: *Barbarians
undress yourself.*
And we undressed.
He was jealous.
Because Barbarians are not syphilitic,
barbarians have healthy blood,
healthy bones and healthy flesh
and a joyous heart.

Barbarians carry heavy burdens
or throw boats across their shoulders.
What do you do with syphilitic gentlemen
in tail-coats?

———

You are like a song.
Your content is impossible
to explain.

A struggle with the submariners
against Slovenian arts.

# A Soft Evening

A soft evening over the Karst.
Excelsior Paper.
A white road.
Vineyards: Refosk.
A willow bush.
A house on wheels.
A piano on two feet.
XYZ.
Wreck. Build.
A white building.
Our aims.
Ay—
Ay—
Death.
Death is coming to console us.
What are the birds up to?
XYZ.

## Kons : X

Sickly inspired French decadence.
What is art?
The Karst, books and loneliness.
Tolstoy: Resurrection.
A student's memories.
Talkative friends of my lonely hours.
Lethargy.
Ljubljana: cemetery of youthful dreams.
Life doesn't much differ from death.
Ljubljana makes people average
or unhappy.
Resist Ljubljana!
For headaches there's aspirin.
Youthful dreams can't die.
I've burned all my memories.
Ljubljana lies at 47° north.
Radić on a republican horse.

# The Arch of Triumph

The Arch of Triumph
Expansions —

K onstructive SPIRIT
   ONSTRUCTIVITY
   ONS

Three entrances:
from one Him
from the second Her
from the third Me

MYSTICISM

# Kons: M

THE CAT.
A tragedy in 3 cramps.
Morning in Trieste.
4 Zeta.
In the shadows it is cold,
in the heart it is still
nice from yesterday's dreams.

Hey, Goldilocks, see
how the dawn is
coming in your
kiss?

## Society is Collapsing

**Society is collapsing**. Are we at fault? We
haven't come to mend. Mending is done by
tailors. We've come to break. A need in my
heart to break. We bring the new. **New**. We
ride on fiery horses. Their manes are forests
on fire. **We are against etiquette**. Etiquette
is rot. We heal with laughter . . . We want to
exhaust you with laughter. We are against
morality. Morality is rotten. We are against
ethics. Our ethics is work. Our ethics is work.
Society is collapsing. It is its own fault. It is
collapsing because it doesn't live. Don't wash
your beard with Eau de Cologne. Go to the
spring in the mountain. The mountain. In
the morning at five. There I will reveal to
you the secret of life. **You. You. You!**

———

Ox horns
above the door.
ARTESIAN WELL
Man No 13

# The Budget

Finances = 0
financial hopes = indeterminate
happiness and strength = enough for three
energy = ∞
despair = 3 × per week
falling in love = every month
debts = indeterminate
hope in the future = ∞
rectilinealibility = a//b

---

Summary = impatient expectation.

# Requiem

Under your wings hide your glow,
squeeze the melody into your chest,
let your passions take a deep rest,
let there be darkness and peace with you.

Farewell bright goals! Farewell without bitterness in the heart!

I am silent at the border post: you, my friends, fly after the stars.

My youth was like a quiet dolina on the Karst, a gorge with a green velvet covering. Its eyes were opened, the sky spilled into them. And a soft wind breathed over its dishevelled hair.

I am a suppressed, unspoken thought. It will never be uttered. I even think it in fright and fear.

And yet this thought is the only one still pulsing in this ragged heart, the only one into which my eyes stare sickened by the insanely flickering film of the present.

And this tattered film is in fact my only brother.

# Notes

*Brinovka*: the fieldfare, also (as in 'Ballad') called the Juniper Bird.

*Burja*: sometimes translated 'Bora' or 'Boria'; a cold Northerly wind blowing down onto the Karst from the Julian Alps.

Ivan Cankar: (1876–1918), a late-Symbolist/early Modernist Slovenian poet, playwright and author.

Karel Čapek: Czech author/dramatist who introduced the robot in his 1921 play *R.U.R.* (Rossum's Universal Robots).

*Dolina*: a depression in the landscape characteristic of the Karst, caused by small collapses or cave-ins in the subterranean limestone.

*Edinost* ('Unity'): a Slovenian political association, and the name of the main Slovene daily newspaper, published in Trieste, the premises of which were attacked several times by Italian fascists in the early 1920s, and finally burnt in 1925.

The Ninth Country: the abode of fairies.

*Refosk*: the name of a grape variety grown extensively in the Karst, and of the red wine made therefrom otherwise known as *Teran*.

SHS (Kraljevina Srbov, Hrvatov in Slovencev): the Kingdom of the Serbs, Croatians and Slovenes.

Stjepan Radić: leader of Hrvatska republikanska seljačka stranka — a Croatian Republican party — at a time of political tension between Slovenes and Croatians in the Kraljevina SHS in 1925–26.

Triglav: the highest mountain in Slovenia, and highest of the Julian Alps.

Trnovo: a neighbourhood in Ljubljana.

Vida, the Beautiful: according to Slovenian legend, a beautiful woman abducted by a Moorish sailor on the Adriatic shore and taken to serve as a wetnurse for the Queen of Spain.

Windelband: Wilhelm Windelband (1848–1915), German philosopher.

Zeta: a brand of cigarettes.

Lightning Source UK Ltd.
Milton Keynes UK
UKHW02f2006080318

319091UK00003B/70/P